Half the Human Race

Susan Utting was born in South London, moved twenty times in forty years, then settled, after a fashion, in Berkshire. Notions of home, identity and where she comes from frequently feature in her writing, and are again explored in this book, as are the shifting lives of other women, the *Half the Human Race* of the title. Susan studied Creative Writing at Sussex University and English with film and drama at Reading University, where she subsequently taught for more than 17 years. Her awards include an Arts Council Laureateship, a Poetry Business Prize, The Berkshire Poetry Prize, The Peterloo Prize and a writing fellowship at Reading's School of English and American Literature. Her poems have been published in *The Times*, *TLS*, *The Independent*, *Forward Book of Poetry*, *The Poetry Review* and *Poems on the Underground*. Her work was selected by the London Poetry Library to be recorded for Poetry International at the South Bank Centre, where it was broadcast with other international poets' work. *Half the Human Race* follows and includes selections from three earlier collections: *Striptease* (Smith/Doorstop), *Houses Without Walls* (Two Rivers Press) and *Fair's Fair* (also TRP).

By the same author:

Fair's Fair, Two Rivers Press (2012)
Houses Without Walls, Two Rivers Press (2006)
Striptease, Smith/Doorstop Books (2001)
Something Small Is Missing, Smith/Doorstop Books (1999)
Scratched Initials, Corridor Press (1997)

Also by Two Rivers Poets:

David Attwooll, *The Sound Ladder* (2015)
Kate Behrens, *The Beholder* (2012)
Kate Behrens, *Man with Bombe Alaska* (2016)
Adrian Blamires, *The Effect of Coastal Processes* (2005)
Adrian Blamires, *The Pang Valley* (2010)
Adrian Blamires & Peter Robinson (eds.), *The Arts of Peace* (2014)
Joseph Butler, *Hearthstone* (2006)
David Cooke, *A Murmuration* (2015)
Terry Cree, *Fruit* (2014)
Jane Draycott and Lesley Saunders, *Christina the Astonishing* (1998)
Jane Draycott, *Tideway* (2002)
Claire Dyer, *Eleven Rooms* (2013)
Claire Dyer, *Interference Effects* (2016)
John Froy, *Eggshell: A Decorator's Notes* (2007)
A. F. Harrold, *Logic and the Heart* (2004)
A. F. Harrold, *Flood* (2009)
A. F. Harrold, *The Point of Inconvenience* (2013)
Ian House, *Cutting the Quick* (2005)
Ian House, *Nothing's Lost* (2014)
Gill Learner, *The Agister's Experiment* (2011)
Gill Learner, *Chill Factor* (2016)
Mairi MacInnes, *Amazing Memories of Childhood, etc.* (2016)
Tom Phillips, *Recreation Ground* (2012)
John Pilling and Peter Robinson (eds.), *The Rilke of Ruth Speirs:
    New Poems, Duino Elegies, Sonnets to Orpheus & Others* (2015)
Peter Robinson, *English Nettles and Other Poems* (2010)
Peter Robinson (ed.), *Reading Poetry: An Anthology* (2011)
Peter Robinson (ed.), *A Mutual Friend: Poems for Charles Dickens* (2012)
Peter Robinson, *Foreigners, Drunks and Babies: Eleven Stories* (2013)
Robert Seatter, *The Book of Snow* (2016)
Lesley Saunders, *Her Leafy Eye* (2009)
Lesley Saunders, *Cloud Camera* (2012)
Jean Watkins, *Scrimshaw* (2013)

Half the Human Race

New and Selected Poems

Susan Utting

First published in the UK in 2017 by Two Rivers Press
7 Denmark Road, Reading RG1 5PA.
www.tworiverspress.com

© Susan Utting 2017

The right of the poet to be identified as the author of the work has been asserted by her in accordance with the Copyright, Designs and Patents Act of 1988.

All rights reserved. No part of this publication may be reproduced, stored in or introduced into a retrieval system, or transmitted, in any form, or by any means (electronic, mechanical, photocopying, recording or otherwise) without the prior written permission of the publisher.

ISBN 978-1-909747-25-8

1 2 3 4 5 6 7 8 9

Two Rivers Press is represented in the UK by Inpress Ltd and distributed by NBNi.

Cover design by Sally Castle with an illustration by Peter Hay
Text design by Nadja Guggi and typeset in Janson and Parisine

Printed and bound in Great Britain by Imprint Digital, Exeter.

*For my daughters,
and their daughters and sons*

Acknowledgements

I would like to thank the editors of the following publications, where some of the New Poems first appeared:

The Times, *The Poetry Review*, *The Interpreter's House*, *Poetry & All That Jazz*, *Poetry News*, *Domestic Cherry 5*, *The Stare's Nest*, *In My Basket I Dream* (University of Reading Creative Arts Anthology 2016), *Separate Ways* (BlueGate), *Lyrical Beats* (Rhythm & Muse), *The Listening Walk* (Bath Poetry Café), *The BlueGate Anthology 2014* (BlueGate), *Drifting Down the Lane: Art & Poetry Explorations* (Blurb), *Hildegard: Visions & Inspiration* (Wyvern Works), *Hands & Wings: Poems for Freedom from Torture* (White Rat Press).

My thanks go to the judges and organisers of the competitions where these new poems were awarded prizes:

Simon Armitage for 'Self Portrait as a Ticked Box' in the McLellan Poetry Competition 2015, Anne-Marie Fyfe for 'Room One' in the Kent & Sussex Poetry Society Competition 2016, Anna Woodford for 'Opening the Windows' in The Poetry Society's 'Getting Out' Competition 2016, Greta Stoddart for 'The Properties of Silk' in the Wells Literature Festival Poetry Competition 2016, and to Wells for The People's Prize.

'Pale' was selected for Bradford-on-Avon Poetry Festival's Poems on a Beermat project. 'Two Mouths' was part of Hilda Sheehan's art installation, *The Queen of Europe*, exhibited at Artiste Gallery, Swindon. 'Then' was chosen by *The Times* newspaper for its Best Love Poems feature. 'Elective Mute' was first published on National Poetry Day 2016 for The Poetry Society's annual Stanza Competition. 'Hill Farmer' was commissioned by Reading Museum to accompany *A Sense of Place*, the exhibition of 20th Century Landscapes at the Madejski Gallery, 2015–6. 'Lip-Reading the Poets' was first published by British Sign Language Interpreters' Agency cSeeker for National Deaf Awareness Week 2016.

I would like to thank all my Reading and Swindon workshop friends and colleagues for their invaluable feedback; and my special thanks go to Maura Dooley and Gillian Clarke for their help and encouragement at the Tŷ Newydd Masterclasses.

Contents

New Poems | 1

Report to the Department of Audiology | 3
The Journal | 4
Self-Portrait as a Ticked Box | 5
What was your name? | 6
Double | 7
Half the Human Race | 8
Two Mouths | 9
Lip-reading the Poets | 10
The Bus Stop Game | 11
Hush-Hush Girl | 12
Selective Mute | 13
Sometimes we feel we take up too much room | 14
Third Time | 15
Products of Conception | 16
The Ones that Got Away | 17
Female of the Species | 18
The Sea Orphan | 19
The Better the Day | 20
Sea View Hotel | 21
Room One | 22
In Hotels | 23
Their Separate Ways | 24
Becoming | 25
Portrait of a Woman | 26
In Praise of Bare-Handed Women | 27
Too Old to Die Young | 28
The Sleeper | 29
Opening the Windows | 30
Night Apples | 31
A Charm Against Dreaming | 32
Then | 33
Sorry | 34
The Tree | 35

The Woman who Fell Over Backwards Trying to See a Bird in a Tree | 36
Moon in a Bucket | 37
Swithin's Bones | 38
Swithin's Miracle | 39
Pale | 40
The Properties of Silk | 41
Wheat | 42
Hill Farmer | 43

From *Striptease* | 45

The Spoon-Maker's Daughter | 47
Condensation | 48
Something Small is Missing | 49
Night Drill | 50
The Florist's Assistant | 51
Striptease | 52
For the Punters | 53
The Bathers of the Ladies' Pond | 54
Hinged Copper Poem Dress | 55
Lolita Paints Her Toenails | 56
The Artist's Model Daydreams | 57
Louise Bourgeois: Recent Work | 58
  i Gallery | 58
  ii Spider | 59
  iii The Couple | 60
Late | 61

From *Houses Without Walls* | 63

Catechism | 65
My Mother's House | 66
Her Bones | 71
Memorial | 72
For Herself | 73
To a Woman at the End of an Affair | 74
Fine | 75
Woodwork | 76
Today's Blue | 77
Noise, Great West Road | 78
Noise, Delaunay's Road | 79
Breaking Even | 80
Legacy | 81
The Woman from Sark | 82
The Amazing Spinning Woman | 83

From *Fair's Fair* | 85

Naked | 87
Girl at the Window | 88
Wanting the Moon | 89
Picture of My Mother as a Young Woman | 90
Fair's Fair | 91
The Things | 92
Lament for Susie Green | 93
Under the Blue Ball | 94
Love, Like Salt | 95
The Sisterhood | 96
The Taxidermist | 97

Notes | 99

New Poems

'Without leaps of imagination or dreaming, we lose the excitement of possibilities. Dreaming, after all, is a form of planning.'

— Gloria Steinem

Report to the Department of Audiology

My skin is glass paper, a gravelly rub, the tips
of my fingers are match heads; my leg-bones
click-clack, syncopate to the floorboards, their
whiplash and skitter. Stairs are a tap-dance,
metal-tipped; there's a hum I'd forgotten,
a knock I can't place, music I don't remember.

I swallow; there's an echo, liquid as liquid,
then high at the back, the plumbing's hi-hatting,
tom-tomming. And my voice! It's a reedy song
– *hush-hush it girl, save it for later* –
For now, plastic bags are maracas, tap water's
Niagara, the plughole's a Looney Toons glug.

Outside, I'm eavesdropping the world,
its chirrup and whoosh, its overhead roar,
its ten o'clock wail, tittle-tattle, its holler
and clank. A single magpie: its dirty croak
is a joy. I scratch an itch and my fingernails
thrill, I'm alight with the noise of myself.

At the flick of a switch I was wired.
Now I've fallen, coup de foudre, a sucker
– *go on, say it girl! out loud!* – a lover
of sound, head-over-heels with cacophony.

The Journal

after Song Dong

The first week was in ink,
broad-nibbed black, each day
a slope to the right, the thin
and thick of copperplate.

The second week was fog
and muffle, a slowing down
of daily round, a 4B graphite
exercise in evening.

Week three was smudgy,
began with charcoal across
sugar paper, then washed
its hands of dark for good.

Week four was scratched
with a pin on wood, each letter
purpled-in with laundry marker,
each day a table-top tattoo.

Then I took up my brush,
dipped and wrote with water
on to stone: letters rippled,
grew to words, to stories.

Years now, stone has held
what I have written, has worn
itself away with listening – water
whispers for me, stone never tells.

Self-Portrait as a Ticked Box

'We have more in common than that which divides us.'
— Jo Cox, MP

I would paint myself green for the luck of the Irish, purple
my mouth for a Bow bell's chime, one arm banded black
for the death of a king, dress in red for the wake of my sister.

For the stones on a South Coast beach I'd wear rubber shoes,
for my seaworthy father a hat made of canvas, cut from a jib.
I'd be sitting up straight, for uncle Joe's Friday night dinners.

At my back I'd sketch bulbfields for Freda and Eddie,
their glasshouses still on the Great Ouse's banks, no floods
but a windmill, broad sails and all, for my grandfathers.

For my foremothers I would put fat Russian dolls, full of dear
little girls on collapsible tables, with linen and crochet hooks,
cooking pots stained with pearl barley, and chicken-bone soup.

I'd be dancing a jig, a mazurka, an old-fashioned waltz, would spin
on blocked toes, paint my feet bloody. I'd be carried away on a longboat,
a horse-drawn cart, hay wain, or curled in a home-crafted coracle.

I would sign myself small, with a borrowed name, in fine rain
from the North, touched with good fortune's red from the far,
Far East, shot with silk, spun out in the West. But here, I must

write myself clear, flat as a Midlands vowel, glottal-stopped,
tick as I'm asked, I must paint myself funeral, statistical, *other*.

What was your name?

My name was a pucker of lips, a moue
made soft by the hiss of a breath.

It was lengthened by names of the dead,
made proper by those in the know.

It kept quiet in the dark, in its tight-lidded
jar it grew vinegar sharp.

My name was a nick in the thumb of a stranger,
a casual thing, borrowed, kept on;

was a keeper of grain, felt the Easterly's chill
and turned itself immigrant, Angle.

My name is the same as it was hitherto: a tongue-slip,
a clatter of keystrokes, a cipher.

Double

Your name is not my name,
you are no-one I can pronounce.

The centres of your eyes are black,
their colour has no name I can remember.

My eyes remember everything:
the key, the lock, the closed door.

Half the Human Race

Say we have tiny, dainty feet that fit,
that tiptoe over broken glass or gravel paths
or decorated egg-shells. Say our ankles are
well-turned, our heels are weapon-sharp.
Say our knees are shocking. Say

our nature's pairing, braising, managing
small things. Say we slapped our clothes
on river stones, we mangled, bleached
and starched, breathed steam and saved
the ends of soap against the shortages. Say

we're sweethearts, dolls with waists and hips
that cannot hold our vital organs, say we're
posable, blow-up generous, bonny, plus-size.
Say nice arse, a lovely pair. Say skin like silk,
like leather; say damaged by the sun. Then say

we're clavicle and fingernail, elbow, nape
and lobe. Say we're tearful. Say we're all
of this and none of it and more, and this
is nothing like the end of it. Say.

Two Mouths

i
Beckett's *Not I* on a screen:
tongue, spittle, gaps, the lot, in close-up
grainy black and white, remembered red.

ii
Below her eyes behind their heart-shaped shades,
Lolita's on a poster,
sucking an everlasting sweetmeat on a stick.

Lip-reading the Poets

for Juliet

More than lips, it's in the whole face,
      meaning beyond the shape of a mouth,
more than puckering *oo*s and grinning *ee*s,
      the open-wides of *ah* and *eye*
the press of *emm* and *bee*.

The whole body signifies –
      steady as a sonnet's pulse
then quick as a stop-frame animation.
      There is no signing woman here
to spell out words, spring out her fingers

to say *beautiful* with everything she's got,
      but still from here I catch
the poignancy of a poet's raised shoulders,
      a torso's earnest forward slope,
the raised chin of a challenge.

The signing woman isn't here
      to sweep her chest – one hand
for *like*, two crossed palms for *love* –
      but still I see her raise her arms
high and wide, jazz-handing her applause.

The Bus Stop Game

We wrote on each other's backs, bored as schoolgirls,
burning to be off and away from this outpost
of a rural county.
                        For the moment stuck, we worked
forefinger-slow, shaping words, one letter at a time
on best friends' backs,
                        over and again until they got it,
then reversed, swapped round to feel the tracing finger
press our shoulder blades
                        to a tingle we could not have named
as thrill. Only our skin knew this was something close to
passion, this shuddering
                        of girls becoming women.

Hush-Hush Girl

Let's hear it for the girl with the
shiny shoes and toes at ten-to-two,
for the bob of her yellow curls,
for her crooked front-tooth gap.

Let's admire the stripes on her palm,
the left-hand devil-possessed one, how
she bit her lip as she smudged and sloped
the wicked way, how she spat and carried on.

Let Miss Meadmore weep for the loss
of her whipping girl, Miss Tolly mourn
a blue serge coat with a twisted belt
and a pair of legs for a flat-hand slap.

I won't let go her crocodile hand in mine,
its grip, the red of its down-to-the-quick;
won't cry out for the hush-hush girl who
went away, for the girl who didn't come back.

Selective Mute

'whereof one cannot speak, keep silent.'
— Wittgenstein

Inside her head she's eloquent, knows
all the answers, words that tumble out
in perfect clause and cadence, words

like *clause* and *cadence*, beautifully
enunciated to herself, alone. Like stories
she makes up, hobgoblin tales where

small girls answer riddles, save lives
of princes tied to trees, win golden
treasure kept in chests and coffers, like

this her life is charmed, she's powerful
as a villainess whose thought-spells
turn a pinching boy to jagged stone,

a chalk-faced mistress to a panting toad,
a matron to a pile of linen, waiting to be
scrubbed and starched, flat-ironed, scorched.

Sometimes we feel we take up too much room

For lack of flesh we pinch our skin,
calculate in inches, blame our bones,
brittle as they are, for their weightiness.

We aspire to a feather's shadow, its glide
away from the sun to somewhere it may live
invisible as clean air, untroubling the world.

Third Time

Simple division, accretion, bundle of cells,
begun at the body's whim, this was nothing
to climb in the loft for, nothing to polish

the chrome of the foldable chassis, buff up
its wheels, bounce for the squeak of its springs –
this was nothing to get out the three-in-one oil for.

This was the one-in-three chance, statistically
average and nothing to patchwork a quilt for.
All I knew were the others, the two who were

tried for, agnostically prayed for, who'd listened,
taken heed of my mantras of *please, please*, the ones
who'd come right. This was a blip in the plan,

one in the eye for the happy, a might-have-been,
could-have-been con trick. This was still
something made out of loving; this was still loss.

Products of Conception

When did you start losing?
I check everything with pockets:
combats, duffels, waterproofs,
full-skirted frocks and boot-cuts.

Have you had pain?
those slippy little slits in wallets,
purses, clutches, holdalls, back-
packs, shiny shoppers.

How much are you losing now?
I go between the sheets, loose-leaf,
polycotton, riffle between the covers,
hard and paperback, duck down, hollofil.

Size of a pea, a cake of soap, a fist?
I dive in black sacks, kerbside green-box,
shuffle the out-tray, in-tray, tip out
the shredder, try to piece words back.

Try not to dwell   total bed-rest   nothing
we can do   everything we could   just need
to tidy up a bit   before you know it   right as rain

Right as a pea, a cake of soap, a clenched fist.

have you had pain   how much
try not to dwell   when did it start?

The Ones that Got Away

I will not pray for you, the gods all being dead,
indifferent or deaf to women's timid exigencies.
I won't apologise, although I'm sorry for your
loss, for your not knowing sisters, yours, such
girls you might have loved.
                        I will not ask you why
you slipped away like that, too soon, too bloody
soon to breathe our air, to carry on the growing.

You have your reasons, so I'll let you go, quiet
as lambs, not a peep or a whimper, while I stay
here, tight-lipped against the *almost* of you,
against its sting, sharp as yesterday, as sure.

Female of the Species

Nile Crocodiles mate in shallow water,
in the dry season, in a thrashing frenzy
after some preliminary rituals. The female

digs a nest in the river bank, close enough
to the river to watch it from the water, not
so close it floods when the river swells.

Here she lays her eggs – sometimes thirty,
sometimes twice as many – covers them with
sand; she leaves them there for ninety days.

A female toad, injected with a woman's urine,
lays eggs: a sign the woman has conceived,
a signal for forty weeks of wondering.

When the crocodile's eggs begin to chirp,
the female hauls herself out of the water,
digs out her young, cracking the shells

to free the slower, weaker ones. Once out,
she tosses them in the air, catches them
in her mouth and, six at a time, carries them

into the water, stays close for weeks
till they disperse along the river. Few survive:
all are prey to large fish, storks and mongooses,

to lizards, other crocodiles and eagles.
To term, or some weeks later, a woman
will give birth to a child, in this instance female,

safely delivered. The woman in this instance
will become a mother, a signal for her world
to tilt forever at a different, sharper angle.

The Sea Orphan

my brother wears sealskins to bubble the deep

I've been trying to learn buoyancy, how to
glide through the water, not breaking its skin
with the kick of my heels, to trust to the air
in my lungs. This is the dream, the one –

my brother wears sealskins to bubble the deep
my sister's a merwoman, fish-tailed and scaled

– where I'm feathered and webbed, wings
folded neat on my back, ready to stretch out
for balance or flight; where my feet know
their purpose, their place under water.

my brother wears sealskins to bubble the deep
my sister's a merwoman, fish-tailed and scaled
my mother, a siren, was loved by a sailor

I am cold, gooseflesh and shudder, un-
feathered, naked, a stone in the water,
afraid for the air in my lungs, homeless
and sick from the salt, raw from its sting.

my brother wears sealskins to bubble the deep
my sister's a merwoman, fish-tailed and scaled
my mother, a siren, was loved by a sailor who fathered
my sea-hungry dreams, my land-weary heart.

The Better the Day

The stones remember
her bones, their shape and weight.
They keep a place for her.

Agnes takes the weight off her scullery, dogsbody feet
of a Sunday, folds up her jacket to cushion the stones,
eases the niggling ache in her back to a breakwater,
settles her angry red hands, her poor sore hands
on her knees. She watches the waves lick the legs
of the pier, lapping them shiny, clean, on a good day
a twinkle of sun, picking them out like music-hall
chorus girls, just for a moment, spot-lit like stars.

Day-out, day-in, the pier stands firm
against the wash and suck of shingle-water,
lap and lash, the sting of brine.

Agnes moves, leans forward from the waist as if
to go, thinks better of it, calls to mind the day:
this is the Lord's Day, set aside for even the likes
of her. She knows it through and through, unblessed
as she is, at best unnoticed or at least chastised,
cursed for her weariness. She'll cling to this
a moment more, before *the better the day*
the better the deed chivvies her back to her duties.

Sun-down, moon-up, the sea reflects the pier,
its scalloped loops of fairy lights that shimmy
in the chop of darkened water, giving back the stars.

Sea View Hotel

Agnes on her knees at the front door steps,
her pail a scum of suds, she scrubs slow
ups and downs, tos and fros over
checkerboard slabs: a white comes clean,
a dusty black gets back its proper dark.

She likes it here, first light before the milk-cart's
clip and chink, before the press and clamour
of the street – just her and the lazy cries of gulls,
her with her quiet daydreams. Both hands

on the scrubbing brush, its wooden back,
she feels the dip of its waisted shape,
jogs the pail to see water ripple a dance,
catch a glint of early sun. Her back's

to the sea but she's at the end of the pier
with the spangled girls, high-stepping legs in a
fishnet line, kicking their way past the footlights'
beam, plumed heads bobbing to a can-can tune.

Agnes rises, stands, dries the backs of her hands
down her apron-sides, tightens its strings, carries
her pail, the brassy tune in her head and the shine
of the chorus line, indoors, down the staff back stairs
to the scullery dark, the dirt of its flagstone floor.

Room One

She tells herself: don't listen to the judder and hum of something
switching on, the silence when it switches off; don't try to guess
the reason for that bleached-out patch of carpet, the choice
of gingham peplums, cut-plastic ceiling lights.

                                            Everywhere
she's in her own light – the mirror gives her back a clouded face,
mist-focussed features. There is a touch of boutique in a tiny disc
of soap in tissue paper, sealed with a designer monogram, marked
best before November five years gone.

She tells herself: don't think of windscreen wipers, taxidermy,
peepholes, focus on the poppies on the coffee mugs, the way
they match the crimson painted walls, how delicate their stems;
forget the black of their daubed hearts.

                                              She stares
at the fixed glass strip of a high window, too high to see
much out of, looks for the tops of trees, for any sort of sky.

In Hotels

It is the third day of a life of hotel rooms,
third day in 107, twin-bedded inland, 4.15.
She's watching slow goods trains with
empty trucks slope past a fastened window.

A knock, a voice – *room service* –
at his brusque *come!* a trolley clatters
with its bow-tied server, its silver
wrapped in linen, china, cold collation.

How late it is, how late, she thinks, looks
out at rough embankments, brick, metal
rails that carry empty trains to elsewhere,

that could carry her a long way off, another
day, another place, an anywhere and soon.

Their Separate Ways

after Eileen Cooper

She hugs herself against the cold,
against the stare of his eyes at her
nakedness, the wrapped curve
of her breast. She has taken off
her face, its love-look – she will
not look back at him, but knows
his left hand's raised to a blessing,
or to a gesture of farewell.

They both know their nakedness
for what it is: it is a small bird
between them, caught up in the cup
of his right hand, a bird with a sharp
beak, untidy feathers, half-stretched
wings about to, struggling, to fly.

Becoming

She catches herself in a stranger's mirror –
her top lip juts, its cupid bow pushed
to a flat shelf. She tries to pucker, purse
for a whistle, to imagine sucking a straw.
Can't. Her bottom lip quivers – she checks
all its tricks, grimaces, gets stuck at a pout.

Back home in the bathroom's double view,
her ears have flattened, shrunk, their lobes
and whorls quite gone, turned tufted, to
pinna-less gaps. Hair feathers a cap,
close to her head, tawny, a white flash
between the eyes, her black beaded eyes.

This is a dream she must finish: to sleep it
away, she huddles back down, is lulled by
the rhythm of window-pane water. Hunger
wakes her, first light. She listens, hears, knows
her brothers' song, their call across cold air.
She stretches the wing of her arm, settles, waits

for her tongue's quiver, its shrill reply.

Portrait of a Woman

after Soutine (1929)

Look at the hands – they're fisted, bare-knuckle
clenched across each other: she's ready,
holding on to something fierce. Or simply
holding on, cross at having to sit still so long,
so long when she has work to do out there, where
real life bends and stretches, arches its back,
carries loaded trays, lays tables, clears away,
runs up and down ill-lit back staircases.

What's clear is the face, its shadows,
pigments and angles; its signals. Hold on
to the downward slope of her eyes, the knit
of her forehead, those twisted, rocky eyebrows.
And oh, the downturn of her mouth! Remember
the jut of her lower lip, its red pout. Feel the dig
of her nails against the skin of her hidden wrist
as she holds, holds on against what's given,

what's been taken from her, what's to come.

In Praise of Bare-Handed Women

'One day, an army of gray-haired women
may quietly take over the earth.'
— Gloria Steinem

You who carry bubbling cooking pots,
lift the lids off scorching pans, who scoop
and dole out steaming nourishment, red-
handed, stoically scarred and blistered.

You who swallow sour milk, at home
among a mist of fruit flies, you who scoff
the rotting apple, pungent, blackening banana,
who clear the rack of flaccid carrots; you who

thrive on other people's left-overs – those
sniffy-nosed rejecters. O plate scrapers!
O relishers of leavings! O this'll-do-me
plucky finishers of gristly bits, I bow down

before your cast-iron stomachs, your
asbestos hands – forgive my flimsiness,
the nesh of my pathetic thumbs, my rheumy
eyes, for I am dazzled by the metal glint of

you, the core of you, its steel, its gold.

Too Old to Die Young

So she splits an apricot, enjoys the look
of the dip that nurses the stone, the way
the stone holds on, leaves its half-moon mark.

There is rain against the window,
a horizontal wind that's flattened fences,
hurled litter from city street to backyard plot.

Trees hold on as far as she can see,
they arch, shiver and lean. The old
protected oak sheds only skinny branches.

Mid-January and the grass keeps growing,
green shoots are early, roses flower late.
The signs are good; the signs are not good.

She bites the apricot, enjoys its bitter flesh,
its velvet skin, saves the stone that will not
split and grow, holds it in her hand to feel

its small moon weight. She watches the oak
stand firm against the gale, the rowan bend with it.

The Sleeper

She sleeps with a knife
beside the bed, her pillow
keeps an eye open.

Between her naked
body and the sheet, the press
of an apple seed.

She wakes, brushes off
slow night, its restless cover,
puts back her old face.

Opening the Windows

after Vilhelm Hamershøi, Interior 1909

June, and the ceremony begins. The catch
on a bedroom frame is first – unlocked,
the handle lifted, stiffened hinge eased
to a different angle.

The hairs on her bare arms stir themselves
a little, do not quite rise – there is no thrill
here, simply air on unaccustomed skin.

'Fresh' is the word for outside air come in,
but she doesn't use it – silence is her way,
breath her language. And so the slow
letting-in continues,

pane by pane, catch, handle, hinge, breath,
air that moves, felt along the blood, like a sip
of iced water, like snow after birchwood heat,

petals fallen on dry earth, their cool
restfulness after all that blowsy flowering.

Night Apples

And she woke to the trees all bare,
the fruit gone from them, as if
a thief had shaken them down
to a blanket spread on the ground,
the rough, root-swallowed ground.

As if they'd been scooped up,
made fast in a woven wool cloth,
four corners knotted and pinned,
slung over a shoulder, the back
blades of a giant, a light-fingered

Atlas, who'd carried them off
in the soft nap of night, under
the cover of this, heat-laden night,
to be scattered, tipped at the feet
of an object of love; to be tasted,

sweet as the kiss of a stranger,
a true kiss, not stolen but gathered.

A Charm Against Dreaming

Not to dream of the ice on the inside of windows. Not to dream of the death of a bird, the petroly sheen of its wings, still warm, the rough pleating of feathers, an after-show dead beat, the plume from a showgirl's headdress.

Not to dream and re-dream the glint of its eye, pin-sharp, a mirror, alive with that look, fixed at the world, un-shuttered, indifferent. Not to dream of its panting heart, curled feet, their quiver and grip on the air. Of the quiet at the still of its heart, ice on the inside of windows, the petroly sheen; a charm against nothing but this and this and nothing between.

Then

There had been candles
and cool jazz
and gentleness.

Then
there was a thin moon
a city fox
a quiet holding of hands.

There should have been
shooting stars
fireworks
a fanfare – at least one
bright, noisy cliché.

Sorry

And I say *sorry, sorry*, I don't know what for.
Perhaps it's just for the kiss that follows, ought
to follow. Or it's that game we played: wooden
men on a board and you'd shout *Sorry!* as you
knocked a rival flying.

Nights are never dark enough to sleep through,
sorry peppers my dreams. I wake myself with it,
hear it said as if by someone else: *sorry, sorry*
to the chink of light, then a curse for the curse
of wakefulness.

I'd like to reel my whole life back, begin again,
but *sorry*'s all I've got – a waking dream, sleep-talk
that gives it all away, fretfulness for unremembered
sins, for everything, forgive me.

The Tree

Because the tree has gone, there is a flood
of light across the floor, there is a view
of roofs and backyard fences shouldering
the weight of whose-is-whose. Because
the tree's been taken while I wasn't there –
there was no chainsaw screech, no fluster
and coo of tetchy pigeon, no easy rhyme for
one for sorrow – the tree's a gap, a lost tooth,
a solitaire unstuck from its old gold claws.

Because the bedroom's lost its summer
flicker, its winter scratch, is soaked in
daylight/streetlight, unstoppable by drape
or slatted blind. Because there is no memory
of the tree's going, I cannot, will not sleep.

The Woman who Fell Over Backwards Trying to See a Bird in a Tree

She heard it first – a flutter and rustle, a call, a song
of sorts, too faint to recognise; too far off and high
to spot a wing tip, coloured breast, the length
of a tail feather. It might have been a little bittern,
crested warbler, a bee-eater or Caspian tern;

a Swainson's thrush, a cedar waxwing, Pacific
golden plover, firecrest, goldcrest or red-footed
falcon. But this was Yorkshire, North Moors earthy,
this was grey-skied mizzle morning, claggy ground,
a blasted landscape, all the mud and grit of home.

She tipped her head back, squinnied up, leant further
back and overbalanced flat; eyes to the muzzy tree top,
under a clearing sky she saw, better than all the crested
fanciness of ornithology, this was something fine:
a clattering charm of jackdaws nesting in a dead tree.

Moon in a Bucket

Moon is full of itself. The bucket
is full of the moon. In the clear shine
of its watery face, moon has fallen
in love with its own circle of light,
has forgotten its proper place.

Ripples fracture moon's dream,
jog its memory of water, remind it,
dark ocean of sky, of home. Ripples
tell moon to cherish its own, keep
faith to familiar seas, each dark
surface a still, unreadable face.

Swithin's Bones

What do we know of the sun, here where the grey is all glower,
plum-purple, charcoal, and sky is no kind of friend, the weather
our unshifting taskmaster. Our trees must be felled, for rills grown
to millraces, brooks become lakes to be dammed, stoppered, held back
by the skin of our aching arms, the burn and sweat of our stabbed backs.

Since they moved his bones far from his wished-for, his common-ground
grave to the sanctified slabs of cathedral cold stone, we have known nothing
of sunlight, of blue, flicker or shine, we are soaked in his sorrow, our pity.

All we know of the sun is absence, betrayal or, worse still, indifference.
Untouched, it has left us here sorry, to grope in the grey, plum-purple,
the charcoal of threatening weather. We are soaked clean of our faith,
fear a new god whose name is *Relentless*, we are learning to chant
his commandments, having given up prayer for this muttered curse.
For the shame of our spoiled crops, drowned homes, poor lumbering beasts,
for all we held sacred and dear, we have given up hope of the sun.

Swithin's Miracle

The workmen called me *crone*, on the bridge on my
way to market, *grandma hen!* they shouted, laughed

when I stumbled, fell. For sport they left their toil
and fell to teasing, snatched my basket from me,

played catch, juggled with my livelihood, my living,
my gold-hearted hens' eggs. For spite they joshed,

threw, caught, dropped, then smashed and trampled
the unspoiled rest to a mess of yolk and pearly slime.

The miracle was his appearing, there and then
like that – his hand raised, eyes fierce at them until

they quietened, stilled, saw what they had done
and feared him. Pity, too, was in his eyes on me.

He helped me to my feet, brushed off my soiled
skirt, set my headshawl straight then knelt to scoop

the mess into my basket till it was filled – not
with grit and ooze and bits of broken shell, but

eggs, whole eggs, straw-flecked and warm
as at that morning's gathering. Then he was gone

and the men set to work again, lowering their heads
as I passed, my own head high, heart brim-full,

my arms strong with the weight of their lovely burden.

Pale

I was taught always to scarf and brim my head, soon learned
to huggermug the dark side of a street, seek alleyways
and parasols, to love a cityscape, its towerblocks, its shade.

Through awninged glass I've watched the worshippers of heat
go out bareheaded, naked-faced at mid-day screwing up their eyes,
revering, relishing the glare. Had I the voice, I'd tell them *lift
a heavy stone, find hidden roots there, flattened flesh grown white*;

I'd have them stumble sun-blind into caves, shine torches
into subterranean pools to see the little fishes glimmer,
iridescent, dart and fleet, beautiful, as pale as sugar

The Properties of Silk

Silk will slip like a dream through an 'o', through
the mouth of a wedding ring taken for gold,
or over and over will fold up its acre of self
to a packet of flight to be tested for strength
by the weight of a man, well-built and ready;

one who believes in its billow, its crinoline belly,
in drift and drag, safe landing dream-time.
A man who knows nothing of bushes and trees
still growing in cities, of spinners and weavers,
looms and cocoons, of traders or dressmakers.

Who won't wear it raw or shot to a shimmer,
slub-weave or watered; but will rescue its
silent-night fall, gather its acre of cloud to a
packet of love, fit for a slip of girl, for a bride.

Wheat

The day her father died she walked
out of the house, down the street,
on past the rec, the corner shop,
the chippy, rows of semis, tarmac
fronts ramshackle with saloons,
estates, transits wedged against
front bays, their netted look-outs.

She just kept going, kept her eyes
ahead, steady as her footfall, as
her heart, her breathing. The sound
of traffic stopped her, a throb and
hum, a rumour carried over still air
like the smudge of downstairs
conversation after lights out.

She stood on the edge of a field,
a field of unripe corn she knew
was *wheat*, but call it what you like
– nobody there to put her right,
to argue the toss of imprecision –
she knew what she meant. Cornfields,
meant to be golden, supposed to

glint and ripple in the sun and breeze,
supposed to be swooped on by swifts,
skylarks, or some other kind of small
bird that chirrups after insects; meant
to be the buzz of insects. Not there.
Dull, cloudy, neither day nor twilight,
not a creature, winged, four-legged,

nothing, not a movement, just
the backing track of a motorway,
the three-lane A to B, and her, the weight
of being someone's daughter, daughter
of a father, behind her. Across the field
something moved, something like a bird
she couldn't name, lifted and was gone.

Hill Farmer

He knew the nips and tucks of hedge and ditch,
the rise and dip of every fell and run; he recognised
the stagger of a lame sheep, the call of a ewe caught
in a thicket, the thin bleat of a birth-wet lamb.

He loved the camber of each field, knew well the ups
and downs of tricky ground – he'd learned to leap its
unexpected drops, would spot the stones that stunt a crop
before they juddered the plough; he had a way with tares.

What he didn't know was when his Gwennie passed,
how cold his heart would turn, how his lope across the
hills would slow and stumble, how wearying the stretch
of his tilled fields, how steep the slope of the meadow.

Or how the milk-cow would turn cantankerous and dry,
the hens forget to lay, the stove turn difficult and acrid,
how thin and rusty water from the yard pump, how
sour its taste on his tongue, how it stung his throat.

They found him in the yard, eyes open wide, fixed
on the sky, a lamb with breech-roped legs across his chest,
the mother by his side, her thin bleat a delicate lament.

Striptease (2001)

'To go naked is the best diguise.'
— Congreve: *The Double Dealer*

The Spoon-Maker's Daughter

My head's too full of memories for my own good:
my father as a young man with blunt finger ends,
his forehead then as smooth as the back of a spoon,
a shaper, a burnisher, a polisher of silver,
alchemical, a turner of dull metal into spoons.

A dozen for a baptism, apostle-faced and fine,
vine leaves for a wedding set, the tracery of
families, arms for the nobility, rank by serried
rank of them laid out on green baize cloth.
His hands had their measure, those blunt finger ends

perfected balances of shaft and bowl, of shoulders
engineered to last – *a lifetime thing, a spoon* –
he'd say, and show me how to see myself reflected
upside down; my father as an old man with blunt finger
ends and a head too full of memories to remember.

Condensation

The way a bead of water stutters down a window pane
then gathers speed each time it touches other drops
until they're streaming down the glass full tilt
together in a single rivulet, reminds me of the way
a bead of water stutters down a window pane then
gathers speed each time it touches other drops
until they're streaming down the glass
full tilt together in a single rivulet.

The way my father always cried at weddings and at
everything the Queen said and when people won
big prizes on a quiz show and whenever any kind of
goal was scored by anyone on either side at any match
played anywhere, reminds me that I've never seen
my mother cry and of the way I never cry at all
at marriages or royalty, at tv jackpot winners
or at sports events unless I am reminded
of the way my father always did.

Something Small is Missing

for afh

So you call, and even your best friend's sleeping
and you don't have a mother, or at least
not the one you need
                right now;
even a nomad stops from time to time,
pitches a tent, hangs a hat,
                      wherever.

So you grieve, for the ones you never knew,
never even wanted – all the ones that
got away, slipped through your
                not fingers,
but those other small things: incompetent
thighs, or was it hearts, or was it just
                          insouciance?

So you look, for that same old crack
bid it shine under your small door –
not in corners: you've had them up to
                          here.
So you settle for all that Gloomy Sunday jazz
don't really know which track to go for or which line it is
                                        that's missing.

Night Drill

Flat on our backs on the lawn, she and I,
squinnying up at the sky, on the qui vive
for a sparkle, a glint through the cloud,
knowing the others were shut-eyed, holding
their breath, willing the doodlebug hum not to
stop, promising God the impossible, just for
the stomach-lurch single-note all-clear again;

we were the only ones there, she and I
with our eyes open wide, flat on our backs
knowing nothing of gutters – all the same,
looking up at the stars, fixing them hard
with our squinnying stare, seeing them then
as if for the first time, knowing it might be,
never quite knowing if this were the last.

The Florist's Assistant

Each day her fingers bleed from picking thorns from
long-stemmed roses, for the sake of other people's
lovers, mothers; she takes her time to bruise and crush
the woody stalks of hothouse blooms, then strips the leaves
below the water line, takes tweezers to remove
each less than perfect petal, every bud gone blind.

For the *gone but not forgotten*, the *sadly missed*,
belov'd in this life, cherished in the next,
she stands on wet stone flags and leans her body
up against the workbench while she wires and hammers,
twists and binds, inhales chrysanthemums gone over,
day-old lilies and the fumes of waterlogged gypsophila.

Striptease

The glow of the tips of cigarettes through smoke,
eyes dead behind the eyes; tits, arse, smiles,
entertainment doesn't change that much –

tradition, hard times, goodtime girls,
feathers, slap and fishnet, sequins on
Britannia, a tableau at the end of the pier

end of an era of keeping still, lying
back and thinking of the Follies,
Moulin Rouge, The Windmill, Archie Rice.

Her mother told her once, before her
wedding night, to keep the mystery alive
keep something back, keep something on –

be slow to let things fall – slip slips
downwards. There's a joke about it:
So she kept her hat on…

Always wash your hands
face and moneybox, keep your knees together
getting out of cars, a glimpse of stocking still

thrills the punters, gets them going, the lads,
the saddoes, and the funny ones, the wags,
dead behind their eyes behind the glow,

through the fat ugly smoke their smiles. Naked.

For the Punters

You don't see them, only hear their clatter, mutter, snigger,
then the whoop when you come on, the urge and whistle
to *get on with it*, go *all the way*. And I go slowly
all the way each night, right there into the glare
of the spot, the glamour-light that turns dust into glitter.

One night I'd like to stop it there, rewind the routine music
and begin again from naked – strip my skin off, peel it down
my shoulders, arms and chest, past waist and hips, unravel it
down either leg, step out, then screw it up and fling it.

Then I'd ease off my flesh and be a bone woman,
they'd see me phosphorescent in the stagelight, dancing
like a puppet jerked on strings, and in the dumbstruck quiet
they'd hear me whistle back and laugh out loud at them.

The Bathers of the Ladies' Pond

Each day before they slip their frocks and stockings off
and naked, slide like knives through satin water,
one by one they shake the chestnut trees and wait
for any peeping Tom or Dick to drop like plums
and scamper bruised and red-faced through
the scratching hedge or squeeze their awkward
bodies out between the fence posts and the wire.

Then all the lazy sidestroke mornings drifting into
breaststroke afternoons, the ladies of the pond take turns
to sit out on the side and listen for a rustle in the shrubs,
a crack of twig, they keep a look out for a glimpse
of collar-white or toecap-brown. Then they take up their
handbag mirrors, flash the sunlight into prying eyes till
dazzled, blinded by the glare, the guilty lookers blunder off
                                             and leg it to the heath.

Hinged Copper Poem Dress

after Lesley Dill's installation for Addressing the Century:
100 Years of Art & Fashion at the Hayward Gallery 1998.

The ifs and buts of it are sharp against my shoulder blades,
at first its run-on lines strike cold against my belly,
buttocks, nipples – all the skin parts that it touches,
then the heat of circulating blood begins the chain reaction:
molecule by agitated molecule it warms to me, and one by one
the curves and hollows of its *o*s and esses, of its *b*s and *y*s –
each letter in the mesh fills up with insulating air.

All day I'm careful, keep away from fires,
sunlight, rain; I smell its metal smell like blood,
feel tiny hinges pinch me, hear it chink each time I move;
each time I breathe words move and change their emphases,
they shift the slant of *I* and *you*, of *then* and *maybe*,
suddenly and *afterwards* – whole phrases, sentences
and stanzas realign themselves, take on new meanings.

                                        And when I dance its skirt
percusses to my rhythm, words fly out forced centrifugal as I spin
and spin and stop – and a caesura drops from one line to the next
and so on downwards in a domino effect, but with the sound
of loose change spilling on a flagstone floor.

When I grow tired of it, worn out with wearing I unlatch
the shoulder fastenings, slip each hasp from out its eye
and let the tinny ripple start; now there's a sound like pennies
stopping spinning in the shiver of it to my ankles, feet, the floor –
a cast off, jagged ring of words to be stepped out of, left for dead;

free of it, I find my body's stippled inky green: a chemistry
of sweat and metal's happened, I'm covered nape to heel with
systematic smudges, hard to read; but let the focus slip a little
and there's something just decipherable – written there, against
the odds, is something like a poem.

Lolita Paints Her Toenails

Strange, pushing the soft pads in
between each toe myself, head down,
wiping the brush on the neck of the pot,
the dip and sweep from quick to tip;

strange at first that my hand shook
a little, took a little time to steady,
relax and get the knack I'd watched
and thought I'd learned.

                       But here, now,
with my knees crook'd and my head down,
my hand on the brush, the dip and sweep
and the peardrop smell as it dries –

this is as close as it gets to knowing
the strange pleasure there is in the act
that's easy now: turning nails to pearls,
to my oyster satin pink instead of his red.

The Artist's Model Daydreams

after Giacometti

My head is a spoon that dips and scoops
fine sugar from a china bowl, remembers
sherbet ochre tongues and the stain on the
tip of a finger shrivelled with sucking.

My face is a flower that turns with the sun
sneaks a look from the edge of a tarmac square,
remembers the scrape and bounce of fivestone chalks
worn smooth and round with playing.

My back is an S that aches on a stool, remembers
the scale of ascending C where thumbs go under,
the broken key and the ring of a fender, bruised
in simple time, by a poker's four-four beating.

My legs are a longcase clock, a pendulum pair
that swings and remembers great aunt afternoons
the rub of a cut-moquette settee, a glimpse
of a beaded muslined jug, and ticking.

Louise Bourgeois: Recent Work

Serpentine Gallery 1998-9

'The sculpture speaks for itself and needs no explanation.
My intentions are not the subject. The object is the subject.
Not a word out of me is needed.'
— Louise Bourgeois 1992

i Gallery

Here, I'm side-lined for looking
all skin and eye, bonesharp sensitive
to angle and the fall of light on cloth,
metal, stone,
     closer, I could slip
small as I am, through a bodkin eye,

the sliver bone that she has split
wide enough for me and her, small
as we are – no explanation, not a word
from either of us,
     we are skin and eye
and bonesharp sensitive together.

ii **Spider** *(steel and mixed media)*

Under her belly
    the cage of her memory
wired with mesh
    one empty chair
a fragment of tapestry

        under the mesh
           not a bone
        or a needle
           neither a spindle
        or thread

out from her belly
    the eight of them
spindle-thin
    witch-fingered
clutching the cage

        the relic cell
           holding its fetishes
        keeping them safe
           close as a keepsake.

iii The Couple *(fabric and knee brace)*

The fine line between embrace and clasp
is smudged, erased in one static move
into a single curve, one shape of knee
on knee, close as fingers in a clenched fist.

Look closer at the fabric – it's been made
by human fingers, stitch on stitch it's finely
knitted; there is a thread to follow through
this easy labyrinth, retrace its path until

you reach the final knot, no need to cut it,
tease it out, one gentle pull will start
the to-and-fro unravelling of thread,
the fine line playing through your fingers

round your winding hand, re-winding hand,
a single curve embracing, clasping air.

Late

The long journey to town
the slow steady flow of the red
the dipped dazzle of on-coming white
and the lights against me time after time
and the stop start, stop start of the struggle to get there, soon.

And over it all a high moon
with a face full of woe, a Wednesday
face if ever there was, scarred by the trail
of a jet, marred by the wisp of a dirty cloud,
the wink of a light in the sky not a star but the tip of a wing.

And the swift journey back,
easy and quick, after the sight
of the pair of them safe – her and her boy;
then a clear road all the way, after the touch
and the fine smell of her smell of him, over it all
a beautiful Wednesday un-clouded moon, perfect and bright,
clever and clear, as full in the eye as the look of a just born child.

Houses Without Walls (2006)

'We are all in the dumps,
 For diamonds are trumps,
 The kittens are gone to St Paul's.
 The babies are bit,
 The moon's in a fit,
 And the houses are built without walls.'
   — Traditional Nursery Rhyme

Catechism

What is your Name?
Who gave you this Name?
What did your Godfathers and Godmothers then for you?

I come from a place with *beech* in its name;
my name then was wished for, dropped
from the mouth of an old woman, fat
as a grandmother, soft, round as an egg.

Conceived in the eye of a sad man,
I was born at the trip of a young woman's
foot, a tumble that rushed me, unready
to air, light, gravity's chill.

I was nourished on milk from the tip
of a spoon, sugar-sweet, thickened
with bread; and crucible tops from soft-
boiled eggs, made yellow, salty with butter.

I grew fat, white as a grub, gurgled,
babbled, spoke, settled for serious talk.
Loquacious, prodigious, I figured the world
in my mouth, made language a loose tooth

to push with my tongue – *cylinder, Hollander,
colander, kiosk,* – I rolled it around,
five years without stopping for breath.
I gorged on its sweet, salt, bitter, sour,

sucked hard on it, bloodied the roof
of my mouth with its acid. I come from
the quiet of a coy girl, dark-eyed, slim
at the waist, a girl in a green dress,

whose name then was chosen by men,
who taught her to lower her eyes, press
her lips, narrow her throat, swallow words
down; who taught me the power of *hush, hush, hush.*

My Mother's House

i
My mother's house is full of birds and lodgers
sitting on the stairs, sleeping underneath the beds
and shinning up the drainpipes at the back;
she's downstairs, cooking on a disconnected stove,
with a cast-iron skillet full of earrings, small pearl
buttons lost from shirts, and silver collar studs.

My mother's wardrobe's full of ball-gowns,
sandwiches and biscuit barrels full of instant coffee,
there's granulated sugar in her dancing shoes
and corned beef in the pockets of her mother's mother's
musquash; she's counting out her trifle dishes, knitting needles,
crochet hooks, the motorcycle magazines and sixpences.

My mother's landing's full of women, queuing for the lodger –
the young one with the torch and cycle clips; she's looking for
an egg-and-bacon pie and a Thermos flask of tea to tide them over,
while the lodgers on the stairs begin a song her father sang,
with choruses, rude verses, all the twiddly bits and harmonies.
They're singing *Susie Green* to her, *we love you Susie Green*,

while she scoops vanilla ice-cream into amber sundae glasses,
adds angelica and violets, tiny roses made of marzipan
and coffee-flavoured biscuits, shaped like fans.

ii
They're in the garden – they've been there
every place she's lived as long as she remembers.
She remembers things from eighty years ago now,
better than from yesterday, ten minutes back
or that scotch mist of time they call *just now*.

The birds are cleverer than clock time –
don't let them in, you'll never get them out,
flocks of them out there, beyond the window,
the ones you can't quite see, that no one else sees;

they're there disguised as dead leaves,
broken seed trays, crocks and stones,
behind the weeds and bushes, in the uncut grass –
whatever tricks they pull they don't fool her,
she's canny, got their number, always spots them.

She double-locks the doors, keeps latches down,
seals off the windows, shoots the bolts at night.
She'd board the fireplace up, but lacks the know-how,
gave his tools away some time back now, or sold them,
can't be sure, is sure she couldn't have, she wouldn't.

And now there's no deep voice to shoo them back,
to clap his hands and curse, all night she hears them
shift and huddle, knows they're watching in the dark,
asleep out there, each one with one eye open.

iii
He's there before her in the early-morning kitchen:
a stranger with a knowing grin, waiting, bold as ninepence,
for her to switch the kettle on. He leans against the sink
and watches, folds his arms and sighs, then tilts his head
and waits for her to turn her back, to turn himself to air.

Some days he's there again at dinner-time, never eats,
moves his lips but never speaks; and when he brings
the children – quiet little things with ringlets,
button boots, old eyes in serious faces – she can't
make out exactly what it is he wants of her.

Lately he's been leaving things: old-fashioned chairs,
fancy tables, unfamiliar knives and forks, stale cake
and dusty ornaments – she used to find her way round
with her eyes shut till he turned up without a *by-your-leave*,
grinning, giving her that look, as if he owned the place.

iv

All night she's dreamt of rowing boats, the heads of dogs
and flotsam bobbing down the street, bedraggled cats
with arched and shivering backs stuck high on rooftops.

She climbs a chair to look out of her window: not a sign
of paving stone or tarmac, the pillar box has gone, the shop
across the street starts two floors up with residential nets.

She watches shaky mirror pictures in a dirty river, tries
to stare them still, to fix them there – *no nearer, higher,
closer* – loses to a kitchen stool that floats past on its side.

She climbs down to a dead phone, a double-bolted door,
no peephole to see out of, to see in through, a muffled
knocker and a disconnected bell. Upstairs, she's safe –

the only safe one left until they come, as come they will,
tramping higher, nearer, closer till they find her there.
She listens; then starts to drag the chair across the room

towards the door, the bolts, the lock, the handle,
imagining its stiffness, the creak of unused hinges,
the draught, the crack of light that might come in.

v

My mother's house is moving down the street:
it's a double-decker bus and she's on top,
she's looking down at Eric cracking jokes,
twinkling his gypsy eyes at the girls; and Phil
done up to the nines, Fred to her Ginger,
wowing the Palais crowd with his fishtail footwork,
scissor steps, and the double reverse spin-turn.

My mother's house is a travelling fair
on the lit-up common between the wars,
before the searchlights came and the lads
all went away; Mollie's there eating Five Boys
chocolate, dragging them back with her spoilsport
whining, scared of the switchback thrills
and the husky call of the helter-skelter man.

My mother's house is shooting the front door bolts,
putting up the towels: it's a snug bar round at the back
and Ron's calling out *last orders, time gents please!*
while she cashes up, turns the optics off,
pours a hefty double with ice and hitches herself
in her sparkly top, to the high red stool for one last
late night, all night lock-in session with the lads.

Her Bones

Her bones have leached themselves to honeycomb,
quiet and unbidden they have given themselves up.

While life was playing out its game of tag,
of kiss-chase, rock-a-bye, releasey-o,

its pantomime charade of chase-the-lady,
close your eyes and count up to a hundred,

ready or not, the witch's footsteps at her back
have sneaked up and have caught her out, unsteady.

While she's watched slips of moon grow fat
and slice themselves away to sickle blades

her bones have thinned to claypipe brittle
till she is a shepherd's crook, a rusty angle-poise,

a number seven; a three-legged hobbler,
story-book bent crone, blind but for the ground

to watch for specks and crumbs, a trail to lead her
back, soft-boned and snug, to where she started.

Memorial

One day she'll plant a tree,
the sort with gaudy summer berries
and flouncy leaves that fall in winter.

She'll decorate its naked arms with scraps
of Spanish lace and lanterns made from
tissue paper, cotton thread and glue.

She'll paint its trunk snow-blizzard white,
(two careful coats) then take her pocket knife
to etch it with initials inside crossword grids.

She'll shower it with confetti made from
artists' cards from galleries, photographs
of long week-ends and holepunch polkadots.

She'll watch it from her window –
like the look of it, the way it nods
as if it knows her; the way it scatters

paper, lace and flakes of blizzard white
that will not melt like snow on warm earth,
                              snow on skin.

For Herself

Today, she will buy tulips for herself, because
she's worth it; from a supermarket tub

of bright white blooms she'll choose her bunch:
tight-budded, sealed in cellophane that crackles

nicely, that will split like silk between
her kitchen scissors' blades. With her knife

she'll cut the stems by inches, at a slant
and clean – today she'll celebrate

the lack of shilly-shally buying tulips
for herself, the absence of *he-loves-me-*

loves-me-not about the petals folded
in their capsuled, green-tipped, calyxed heads.

And time will pass and she will watch for them
to open, convent-waxy, first-communion-frocked,

cool and smooth as the vase she'll choose for them,
white as the perfect walls they'll blend against.

But when they open they'll be shocking yellow, frilled
and fluted at the edges, they'll be vulgar-skirted

chorus girls, and she'll laugh at herself, to herself
each time she passes, sees them opening their rude

mouths wider, wider still until they're flaunting
their sex at her, their dusty little bright-heart centres

and she'll throw back her head and laugh out loud
for buying tulips, tight white tulips, for herself.

To a Woman at the End of an Affair

Forget Delilah: remember all the lovers you will leave,
forget the few who will leave you, remember then
the smell of just washed hair, the squeak between
somebody else's fingers, the towel cape, clipped
at the front like a bunch of paid-off cheque stubs.

Feel the tug of the comb, the teasing through
to smooth, the cold curtain across your face,
the wait. There is a pleasure in the sound of sharp steel
cutting wet hair, like a guillotine through heavy paper
or your mother's pattern scissors cutting taffeta.

This is what we do: we close our eyes and dream a little,
wake and shake our shingled heads, our bobs and urchins,
smile and thank reflected faces, nod at our accomplices
and walk away relieved, of something; *light-headed*'s
not the word for it, exactly, simply there's a lightness

in our tread, a softening of shoulders, neck, our arms
swing easier, our naked foreheads smooth, our eyes –
remember this – each time, our eyes become a little clearer.

Fine

Then some days loss is tangible as the ice
you chip and claw at till your fingers numb,
go sticky and red. Or it's shrill

as the scream of a scalded child
that won't be hushed, hears its own voice
echo far off, make a sound like someone else.

Like a glass that's rinsed and polished back
to a glint, to ring at a finger's flick,
this is fine; as fine as the flutter

under the bone-cage place where
the muscle you once called heart is.

Woodwork

I'm building a box: not quick-assembled
with an Allen key and diagram, not pine
or MDF or even beech veneer, this one
is patina'd and grained in walnut,
dovetailed, countersunk and bevelled,
heavy-lidded, hinged with solid brass.

It's big: just big enough to hold
New York, a pilgrimage to Northern Spain,
a framed collage of cheapday travel cards
to castles; and a house with elbow-room
for two, sky windows and the sound
of Chinese wind chimes telling tales.

The picture of a person lying
at a crossroads will fit in beside
the sound his body made as it hit metal
and the way it trembled, bled along
with all the promises the morning
had just made about its afternoon.

The lid and body marry perfectly,
a soft click as the catch slips
into place – no need for chains
or padlocks; tap its sides and listen,
clench your fist and knock to hear
its low-pitched, empty echo.

Today's Blue

Today's blue's nothing turquoise, it does not
shift in the light from duck-egg bright to aqua,
it is not a patch of sky to mend a sailor's trousers
or the uniform of girls let out in crocodiles, on pre-set
routes through Mellor's Park on Wednesday afternoons.

It's not indelible on children's tongues, or carbon
smudged on sweaty palms and touch-type fingertips,
nor is it jazzy/sad mood indigo for something small
you'll always miss but never really had; today's blue
is a memory of worsted cloth, tacked long and loose,

worn inside out, marked white with broken lines
of tailor's chalk. It is a man cross-legged on a table
in a backroom; it is not my father, though he's there
and with me and would understand the weft and warp,
the mesh of yarn, tight-woven to a blue so dark

you'd call it black; that he'd call *midnight*.

Noise, Great West Road

We knew that it wasn't the wind,
but the sound of the underground train
coming up for the air, over the wall
at the end of our area yard.

We lived semi-basemented, coal-holed
and railinged, at home to the overhead
drumming of boots from a neighbour
gone Spanish for love;

                        we were snug,
huggermug with West Indian weddings,
chiropractors and washing-line underwear
thieves; with paraffin stoves that caught fire,

doorstep shit, corner-shop pregnancies,
men who turned out to be women, bottle-
fight pubs, one-armed bandits that flashed
to the smashing of glass while the landlord

kept serving, and we kept on hearing
the Underground whooshing, as windrush.

Noise, Delaunay's Road

Not lead shot sprayed from a gun against a wall
or rattling on a plate from a scoop of pigeon stew,
not dried peas spilling on the old cracked lino
of the backroom wash-house, unconverted scullery,

not hailstones on the windscreen of the pick-up van
we painted red from rusty blue, but gravel
on a bedroom window, early hours of Sunday,
because we haven't got a front door bell.

Because you haven't got, don't need, a key
because I'm always there; because tonight
I'm not up, ready with an ear, a body, with a finger
on the latch to let you in because I've fallen,

dreaming of disasters, to a fitful sleep, deep
enough to nightmare on through theatre whispers,
half-shouts, half-cut anger; but not through gravel
fistfuls at the window till I'm up and you are in

and I am taking down fine wedding china, gold-rimmed
white, from off the shelves in the backroom wash-house,
unconverted scullery, till the old cracked lino's covered
with a beach of jagged rocks and tiny china gravel chips.

Breaking Even

I bruise easily,
heal fast – it's a family thing,
this taut, thickening skin.

Legacy

I leave you the green silk dress that wasn't silk
but shivered like it was, slipped easy as an arm
around a neck for the last slow dance at a go-down
jazz club night; I leave you a chiffon scarf

and Chemistry, the chill of the attic room we chafed in,
the basements full of strangers-into-friends
and the fire that blazed in the last one, one September
to come home to, weary, punch-drunk, bundle-laden.

I leave you the strange enthusiastic neighbour,
expert in the ways of trains and traffic lights,
and the jazz man with no sense of rhythm, the lie
of perfect pitch, our syncopating spoons and bones.

I leave you a singer with too many words to the line,
who made them fit and mean between the wheeze of chords,
the thrill of sitting there not shouting *Judas* while
the others upped and left. I leave you poetry & jazz,

the angst of anger, bears & squirrels, the kitchen sink
of cinema, the grainy grey of subtitles, the books
we'd *really read* piled round the edge of the room,
that rug, those ankle-bruising chairs, the suck of wind

that slammed the door, that smashed the glass, the sound
as it shattered, fell, the pick of our bare feet through it.

The Woman from Sark

What she missed was the sound of her own tongue,
that easy patois everyone knew, where everyone knew
who she was like the lapping of water, the look
of the sea, familiar and full in the eye as a friend,
cousin, kinswoman, relative, reconciled enemy.

That, and the clean mist, the soft-focus mizzle
that left her with salt on her skin and a fresh
damp in her bones to be warmed by the ashfire
of home, fed from a table she knew like the lines
on her mother's face, like her brother's voice.

Here there were streets to be wandered at night,
the echo of footfall on hard ground, permanent light
and air that grubbied her skin while she searched
for a river, a dark edge to watch for a flicker
of tidal shift, for a sign, for a voice she knew.

The Amazing Spinning Woman

I push against the air, a swimmer
without water, I am a caught fish
on a barbless hook

high above the mosaic floor
where chips of zigzag pattern
blur to watercolour pale

underneath an amber roof, cheek
by jowl with gilded cornice, jade
green arch and barley-sugar twist.

My head is tilted to an angle,
sharp against the soft curves
of the ceiling, and my hair

falls back – a fur of hair,
the brush of a fox
on the back of my neck.

I know the broidered garlands,
hand-stitched swags across my belly
quiver as my body stiffens;

I grit my teeth on metal,
tighten jaw and neck, a flick
to jerk the wire to start the push,

the slow-turn spin; hold on
and push against the air,
push harder, wider, faster,

till I'm flying, till
I am a sparkle-hoop
against a painted sky.

Fair's Fair (2012)

'Of lives, the lucid.
Of deaths, the rapid.'
— Berthold Brecht, from *Orge's List of Wishes*

Naked

More than I'd seen before, more
than a rabbit, skinned by the sleight
of a butcher's hands, much more than

the deft red of his wrists. More than
a plucked bird on a hook like a capital
ess in a copperplate book and more

than a grandmother's mouth stripped
of its keyboard, its click and grin, more
than the gloss of her chopperless gums.

More than his startled skin, its gooseflesh
and quiver, the gristle that made him *boy*,
more than his ears without their pink wires,

more than all that, lacking their circles
of glass, the blur and fuzz of their squint
looking back at me, more naked than Adam
after the apple: the boy in the bathroom's eyes.

Girl at the Window

after Oskar Kokoschka

Inside, the bird in its cage swings
on its swing, small as a wren but black
as a rook, no tongue in its head to sing,
no glint in its eye for the weather.

Outside there's a full moon touched
by clouds and the stars are out like
Christmas; trees droop with the weight
of their leaves, and still no rain has fallen.

The girl leans on the sill, half out,
half in, the book on her lap lies open,
her face is pale as a winter moon,
her hands crossed neat as wings.

She tilts on her stool, stares out,
the words in her head unspoken;
small as a wren, black as a rook
the bird in its cage swings on.

Wanting the Moon

'If I could choose
Freely in that great treasure-house
Anything from any shelf,
I would give you back yourself...'
— Edward Thomas

The sky is as wide as a sleepless night
and I miss the moon. I want it out,
the whole of its fat face, flat
as a tin badge with a lopsided smile.

Like a child who climbs on a roof,
clings to the stack of the chimney
and weeps till her tears loosen the mortar,
unsteady the bricks, turn soot to a salt-water
trickle that drip, drips on the stubborn hearth,
I want the moon.

         I want it to sweep your face
bright as a searchlight, to find you, head tilted,
chin up, lips making words at the ink of the sky;
I want the moon to know what it is you are saying.

Picture of My Mother
as a Young Woman

Look at her flirt in her flash-vivid bolero,
lash-flutter, hair-flick and kiss-me-soft smile:
she's wearing the sequins and satin, gold thread
embroidery, pleated-sleeved, edge-to-edge moiré
coatee, that was bargained-for, haggled and smuggled,
swaddled in khaki, shouldered by kitbag through
mud-field and cart-track, held river-high, ocean-dry,
sky-dropped and army-truck juddered away from
the home-fire promisers, gunfire & bonhomie.
    Look at her, girlish as romance, done up
to kill in the glitter-bright bolero, sweet-hearted,
rescued and true as a love-token, trophy or spoil.

Fair's Fair

'We are not all able to do all things.'
— Virgil, *Eclogues viii*

Lend me your quickstep twinkle, your Highland Schottische
and I'll lend you the flex of my knees, my steady toes, my hop
for your shuffle, your ballet fingers for my bitten thumbs.

For your stockpot skim, take the taste on my tongue – it's
all yours – and I'll give you a go with the bite of my teeth,
my jaws for your chomp on a liquorice log and a whole tray

of nut brittle – I'll give you the hammer, throw in the brass dog
for the walnuts. If you lend me your marzipan basket of flowers,
the weave and flow of your piping-bag nozzle, your spatula's lick

and the last scrape of your caterer's bowl, I'll bring you an unshaken
bottle of Jersey gold-top and a stiff drink in a straight glass, pink
elephant ice for a triple, nudged out from the blind eye of the optic.

Lend me your strong crop, its pepper-and-salt, and I'll lend you
my pump-water mouse, my pale cheek for your cock-a-snook. Give me
your tall larder of tales, the false and the true and the half-way there:

I'll give them the cut of my jib, my threading eye for your invisible darn.

The Things

For want of a foot, the shoe wept
like a babe in the crook of the wrong
woman's arm, it wouldn't be cradled
but struggled, arched itself, threw back
its tongue, dug in its heel, would not
be swayed, lullabied, softened.

For want of a fist, the glove snivelled,
skinnied itself to a pale thing, a shadow
of thumb, fore, thimble, ring, little,
to skin without bone, papery hide without
flesh. For want of a body the frocks sulked,
shouldered their hangers resentful as sinners

kept in, grounded away from the glitterball;
for want of a generous hip, for a bosom
to swathe, for a soft crease to reveal,
for a valley, a silk-stockinged thigh to flash
through their slashes, an ankle or calf
to show off their kick pleats, for want

of a woman with meat on her bones
they frayed, threadbared, tarnished,
rusted themselves to an obsolete regiment.
For want of some rhythm, muscle,
blood, for want of a voice, the things
stilled themselves, quietened; fell apart.

Lament for Susie Green

No more the wicked tongue, the lizard skin shoes,
the cerise and black, no more the oyster and blue;

no more the filthy look, the thrupenny bits, no silver
or bronze, no more sixpence-suspenders, no lash-glitter.

No more the cochineal bottle, no bitters, no sauce, no
salt-pinch, no ice-chink, no backchat and no maraschino;

no more the pussyfoot kick, no more swift ones, no halves,
no more two fingers, no specials or jugs, no straight glasses.

No red hat, no fur coat, no Chantilly lace, no pins in the mouth,
no grosgrain or petersham, frogging or darting, no snowing-down-south.

No more the dog-see-the-rabbit, no go joe, no rabbit, no cricket, no score,
no peplum or jabot, gadget or slingback, no hip-shimmy heel spin; no more.

Under the Blue Ball

Here's where the glittering queen bee descends
every night, with a creak from the rickety spiral,
ducks under the lintel where strangers' heads crack.

Here's where curmudgeons guard seats by the fire,
the inglenook regulars tapping their pipes out
where roll-ups and full strength have kippered the walls,

where bluebottles buzz in with stable lads steaming
like horses; where bets are laid, arrows thud, dominoes clatter
and cribbage gets rowdy with *one-for-his-nob* of a Friday.

When the bitter gets lively a knife skims the froth, the mild's
dark and dangerous, tasty as treacle, the Stingo's a kick to it,
Barley Wine's kept out the back for the brave or the foolish.

At last orders the landlady holds up the ceiling, wedges the door back
to let out the fug, and over the road the dead shake their headstones
to Country & Western played on the jukebox, or Victor Silvester

slipped in by the landlord. While invisible feet tread the boards
overhead, the hands of the long-dead lift latches at midnight
to join in the lock-in with hippies and huntsmen, jowl by cheeking

with blind-eyed law officers, majors and grease-monkeys,
chippies and smallholders. Butcher and cheese-maker, flagstone
and fag-ash, here's the whole world under rafter and roof-thatch.

Love, Like Salt

'What shall Cordelia do? Love, and be silent.'
King Lear, Act I Sc.i

Like sand through the nip of a waisted glass, salt
pools on a dark plate and waits – the old conceit –
for you to make your mark: tine-lines, knife-edge
asterisks, the swirls the tip of your finger chooses.

Like a father's test – *How much?* a daughter's sure reply –
Like fresh meat needs salt, love's necessary as air, as
oxygen to a blue flame, as a vital pinch to keep you
safe from the wrath of devils you don't believe in.

But here's unholy salt on a plate, tap it back to flat,
to freshly fallen, clean-sheet white, imagine its sting
on the tip of your tongue, dip your finger in and wait.

Now make your mark, insignificant rune, that easy
hieroglyph, sweet conceit, that love will understand.

The Sisterhood

We are the canny measurers, controllers of the scales,
we set the tables, clear them, wash and wipe up,
dutiful as the shadows sewn to our heels.

A drop of vinegar to seal a cracked egg at a rolling boil,
a sprinkle of flour to cure a curdled creaming,
a metal spoon to cut & fold, to keep in air; we know

the energy it takes to whisk whites to the soft-peak stage,
the pinch of salt that's a trick of our mothers' trade
picked up at elbow, learned at marble slab, by syrup tin.

Thinner, paler than our mothers, we won't age like them
but shrink like sponges, grow down on our faces as we make
each day an empty bowl, a grain of rice saved up for,

a purple fruit to hold in the mouth before we bite, release
the stain, discover safe flesh and the hard of a stone to keep,
high and husbanded, against our puckered cheeks.

The Taxidermist

Most times it's knowing when to stop, to leave it,
to let go's the hardest bit; but this time something
ticks inside his chest. A small flip-flutter
and he's laying down his grooming brush,
standing back to look at hide and flank, at legs
as delicate as wishbones, those tricky, dainty hooves.

Glossed eyes like alleys shine at him, he knows
their fringes, lash by lash positioned by his steady hand
and sees that it is good, is finished. He folds his arms
across his chest and leans the weight of all his weariness
down through his heels, relieves the slow ache in his back
and sees that this is something other than his making, this

swell and symmetry of belly stripes that shift, as if a breath
is being taken, as if, somewhere inside, a heart is ticking.

Notes

I am grateful to Smith/Doorstop Books for their kind permission to reproduce work from *Striptease*, which also includes some edited and selected poems from *Something Small is Missing*, a winner in The Poetry Business Pamphlet Competition.

The words quoted on page 5 are taken from Labour MP Jo Cox's maiden speech to parliament on 3 June 2015. Jo Cox was MP for the Yorkshire constituency of Batley and Spen. She died on 17 June 2016, after being shot and stabbed in the street.

Quotations in the Louise Bourgeois sequence are from *Behind the Tapestry*, Mari-Laure Bernadac, for the Serpentine Gallery, London.

'For The Punters' was selected for inclusion in the 2015 Bloodaxe anthology *Hallelujah for 50ft Women*; 'The Florist's Assistant' for the 2006 Arrowhead Press anthology *Images of Women by Contemporary Women Poets*; 'The Spoon-Maker's Daughter' for the 2000 Enitharmon anthology *Parents*. 'The Artist's Model Daydreams' was first featured in the *Independent on Sunday*.

Some of the poems from *Houses Without Walls* were first published in *The Daily Telegraph Arvon International Anthology*, *New Welsh Review*, *Second Light* and *Mslexia Magazine*. 'Legacy' was included in *The Captain's Tower*, an anthology of poems celebrating Bob Dylan at seventy, published by Seren. 'Woodwork' was featured in the *Independent on Sunday* and included in the Forward Prize Book of Poetry 2007.

My thanks are also due to the editors of *The Times Literary Supplement*, *The North*, *Ink Sweat & Tears*, *Kaleidoscope* (Cinnamon Press), *Reading Poetry* (Two Rivers Press) where some of the poems from *Fair's Fair* were first published. 'Under the Blue Ball' won the Peterloo Poetry Prize 2007.

Two Rivers Press has been publishing in and about Reading since 1994.
Founded by the artist Peter Hay (1951–2003), the press continues
to delight readers, local and further afield, with its varied list
of individually designed, thought-provoking books.